Ella's
kitchen

a tiny taste of

the
Cook
Book

yummy recipes to inspire big and little cooks

hamlyn

For Ella and Paddy who inspire us every day.
And for all of their generation – may good
food bring joy throughout your lives.

Paul + Alison Lindley

This special edition published
in Great Britain in 2019 by Hamlyn,
an imprint of Octopus Publishing Group Ltd
Carmelite House
50 Victoria Embankment
London EC4Y 0DZ
www.octopusbooks.co.uk

An Hachette UK Company
www.hachette.co.uk

ISBN 9780600636748

A CIP catalogue record for this book is available from the
British Library.

Typeset in Cooper Light and Ella's Kitchen

Printed and bound in the Czech Republic

Created by Ella's Kitchen and Harris + Wilson

10 9 8 7 6 5 4 3 2

Design and styling: Anita Mangan
Photographer: Jonathan Cherry
Art direction: Sarah Ford
Managing editor: Judy Barratt
Design assistant: Abigail Read
Assistant production manager: Lucy Carter
Production controller: Grace O'Byrne
Food stylist: Vicki Savage & Jayne Cross
Recipe testing: Emma Jane Frost & Nicola Graimes

Disclaimer

A few recipes include nuts and nut derivatives. Anyone
with a known nut allergy must avoid these. Children
under the age of three with a family history of nut allergy,
asthma, eczema or any type of allergy are also advised
to avoid eating dishes that contain nuts.

Some recipes contain honey. It is advised not to feed
honey to children under 12 months old.

Every care should be taken when cooking with and for
children. Neither the author, the contributors nor the
publisher can accept any liability for any consequences
arising from the use of this book, or the information
contained herein.

Publisher's notes

Standard level spoon measures are used in the recipes:
1 tablespoon = one 15 ml spoon
1 teaspoon = one 5 ml spoon

Both metric and imperial measurements are given for the
recipes. Use one set of measures only, not a mixture of both.

Ovens should be preheated to the specified temperature.
If using a fan-assisted oven, follow the manufacturer's
instructions for adjusting the time and temperature.

Medium eggs have been used throughout, unless
otherwise specified. Herbs are fresh, unless otherwise
specified. Use low-salt stock, and avoid adding salt to
recipes altogether.

Certified

B Corporation

We're super proud to be a certified B Corporation
We passionately believe that businesses can and should be a force
for good, so that's why we joined the B Corp movement.

B Corps aspire not only to be the best in the world but the best
for the world.

As members of B Corp we actively contribute to solving social
and environmental problems as well as making sure that we are
a super tip-top employer which promotes the wellbeing of our
people.

It's what we've always been about, but now we have lots of other
friends in the business community who think that way too.

And we're passionate about leading the movement in the UK to
encourage other business to become B Corps too, because then
the world will be an even better place.

Contents

Foreword by Ella's dad.................................4

A bit about using this book...................5

Our cook book..6

First foods for tiny taste buds.............8

From mush to mash + beyond.................10

 Yummy lunches + speedy snacks.............12

 Dee-licious dinners................................24

 Perfect puds + scrummy treats.............46

Foreword by Ella's dad

My wife Alison and I became first-time parents when our daughter Ella was born. The new responsibility, the sense of fulfilment and the unlimited outpouring of love are – I'm sure – felt by virtually every new parent. Parenthood really is life-changing. By the time our son Paddy was born, I'd been an active father for three years – and I loved it.

I experienced first-hand the challenges of weaning and the issues involved with introducing two babies (and then toddlers) to new foods. Ella, like the vast majority of little ones, was selective about what she wanted to try, often with no consistency from one day to the next. My solution was to do what I do best: to be silly and childlike. I thought up food-based games. I tried to encourage her to look at her food, and to touch it, smell it and even listen to it, before finally eating it. I invented stories and made up songs; I created imaginary friends and performed 'magic'. I turned mealtimes into events that were messy, noisy and interactive. Ella laughed and I laughed. Best of all, Ella showed willingness to experiment with and enjoy her food. My efforts worked with Paddy, too.

Then, I had my 'lightbulb' moment: healthy food could be – and should be – fun for young kids. This single notion was to be the inspiration for Ella's Kitchen. I gave up my job and set about creating a range of foods for babies, toddlers and young children. I wanted to develop a brand that would bring together three elements that often work against each other in prepared children's food: healthiness, handiness and fun.

At Ella's we always try to look at life from a child's point of view – with an open mind and with all our senses. My strong belief is that the more a young child is involved with his or her food – whether that's choosing it, preparing it, playing with it or eating it independently – the more likely he or she is to give it a try and to go on to enjoy it. With such a positive start, children are far more likely to grow up to have a healthy attitude not just towards mealtimes, but towards their whole diet and overall wellbeing, too.

We've created this book to build further on the Ella's Kitchen ethos – to help even the youngest of children develop healthy eating habits that will last their lifetime. I hope that it will give you and your family far more than recipes for fantastic children's food. I hope that the shared experience of creating dishes together – from making the shopping list and buying and preparing the ingredients to discovering how they feel and spotting their rainbow of colours – will help to strengthen your bond. The ultimate expression of this bond is when you sit down to eat together with big smiles, enjoying the meal that you have created.

Our Ella's Kitchen family has had great fun experimenting as we've developed the ideas for this book. Now that it has found its way to your family kitchen, I hope that your mealtime experiences are equally good!

Keep smiling

Paul

Paul, Ella's dad x
Follow me on Twitter: @Paul_Lindley

A bit about using this book

We hope that this book is far more than just a cook book. It's about encouraging your children to embark upon a lifetime's adventure with food. As you involve them in every step of the cooking process, you'll help them to develop food confidence.

Their curiosity will turn them into excited culinary explorers – they'll want to smell, touch and taste the ingredients, and they'll love how foods transform during cooking.

By taking time to follow a recipe together, you are sharing quality time during which you laugh together, enjoy each other's company *and* make something yummy.

Key to icons

At the top of every recipe you'll find a combination of the following icons to help make cooking for, and with, your little ones as easy as it can be.

makes

How many pieces the recipe makes

serves

How many children the recipe serves

serves

adults + kids

How many adults and children this family recipe serves

prep

How long the ingredients take to prepare

cook

How long the recipe takes to cook

Recipes that are easy to mash with a fork for babies over 7 months old

Recipes that can be frozen

5

Our cook book

From the beginning

If you're a first-time parent embarking upon weaning, take a look at our simple weaning guide on pages 8–9. Our tips provide the essence of how to introduce an exciting array of foods to your baby from their first mouthfuls. If you have a toddler and a baby and want to make meals that will accommodate both, look out for the 'easy to mash' icon (see page 5), which flags up the recipes that are also great to mash for your tiny family members.

Getting stuck in

Tots and toddlers make wonderful helpers, and at Ella's we believe that messiness is all part of the fun: there's lots to stir, mix, squish, pour, squeeze and decorate. We love it when little fingers are prepared to feel the textures of different foods during the cooking process and then make foods look beautiful on the plate – even if that's just arranging fruit slices in a pattern. Lots of the recipes have suggestions for how little ones can help.

Saving time

We know you're busy, so it's been really important to us that we provide recipes that are suitable for your lifestyle. They've all come from parents like you and have been road-tested by Ella's Kitchen families and friends. Wherever we can, we've included handy hints and shortcuts.

Sensible shopping lists

All the recipes in the book use healthy ingredients. Our team of nutritionists has selected and approved every one to ensure that you can provide your children with a nourishing diet. We use less sugar and fewer sugary ingredients, and avoid salt whenever possible. Instead, we season with a range of herbs and spices. Whenever you can, use low-salt or no-salt versions of stock cubes and other ingredients that might have salt in them.

We recommend that you use organic foods, especially for the fresh ingredients. We believe that organic farmers produce their foods using the purest farming standards.

We've tried to ensure that the recipes call for ingredients that you can find easily. All should be available in your local supermarket, and you may even already have lots of them in your cupboards.

We believe that to have a truly healthy relationship with food, children should never feel guilty or awkward about anything they eat. Healthy puddings – and treats for special occasions – are fine, and all our sweet recipes minimise the use of refined sugar.

Freezer friendly

Your freezer is your friend when feeding a family. Use it well and on busy days it will keep you fed with almost zero effort. Look for the freezer icon (see page 5) on recipes in this book that can be frozen.

Freeze food in a freezer set at -18°C (0°F). Meat dishes will freeze safely for up to four weeks; vegetarian dishes (including fruit pies), cakes and biscuits can freeze for up to three months. Always label your foods with the date of freezing. When defrosting, always do so covered in the fridge, or in an airtight container submersed in cold water, or in a microwave. Eat, cook or reheat foods (as appropriate) as soon as they are defrosted. When reheating, always do so until piping hot all the way through. Do not refreeze.

Eat a rainbow

Exploring different colours in food is not just about creating excitement – eating fruit and vegtables in all the colours of the rainbow will give your baby a wide range of vitamins and minerals to help their body grow and develop.

Here's our rainbow of favourite foods:

Red: Cherry, cranberry, pepper, radish, raspberry, red onion, strawberry, tomato

Orange: Apricot, butternut squash, carrot, mango, orange, papaya, peach, pepper, pumpkin, sweet potato

Yellow: Banana, lemon, parsnip, pineapple, starfruit

Green: Apple, artichoke, asparagus, broccoli, cabbage, courgette, grape, kiwi, lime, pear, spinach

Blue: Blueberry

Purple: Beetroot, blackberry, blackcurrant, grape, plum

Colour a rainbow! Which colours of fruit and veg has your little one eaten this week? Make a picture using those colours.

The wheel of scrummy goodness

It's good to introduce children to the idea that food helps us grow and gives us energy. Use this wheel as a starting point to teach your toddler about the nutrients that help keep him or her healthy.

Vitamin A to help you see

Vitamin C for healthy gums

Iron for a healthy brain

B-vitamins for bouncy energy

Calcium for strong bones

Zinc for immunity

First foods for tiny taste buds

1

When to wean

All babies are different – some may be ready for solid foods earlier than others, and some will take to weaning more quickly. Department of Health recommendations are to start weaning around the age of 6 months but never before 17 weeks.

Look for signs that your baby is ready to wean. They should be able to sit up and hold their head steady, and put an object, like a spoon, into their mouth accurately. Even then, if they push food back out with their tongue, wait a week and try again.

Check with your health visitor if you are offering your baby food before they turn 6 months of age (but after 17 weeks).

2

Ready, steady, go!

Little by little

When you begin weaning, offer food at a time when your little one is not too tired or hungry – in the middle of, or just after, a daytime milk feed is a good idea.

Baby knows best

Most babies know when they've had enough to eat. If your little one doesn't seem to want any more, don't force the issue. You'll know they have had enough when they clamp their mouth shut, push away the bowl or spoon, or turn their head away.

Smoothly does it

Smooth purées give the best texture for tiny tummies. Veggies and hard fruits (such as apples) will need to be peeled, chopped, then steamed or boiled until soft before you blend them; soft fruits (such as bananas) can be blended straight away.

Model parent

Try to eat with your little one as much as you can so they can learn to copy you. Show them how yummy you think veggies are!

3

Veg it, switch it, repeat it

Babies have 30,000 taste buds in their tiny mouths – that's three times more than grown-ups – so new food is big news.

One by one

Introducing single veg tastes followed by pure veg blends early on in weaning gets tiny tastebuds used to savoury flavours. Get your little ones loving a variety of tastes with a rainbow of veggies. It can take up to eight tries for your little one to enjoy a new food. So keep trying!

First weeks of weaning

Here is a handy little planner for the first few weeks of weaning. But remember, this is just a guide: follow your baby's lead and be led by his or her appetite.

Week 1: Once a day

Try 1–2 spoonfuls of purée just after your baby's lunchtime milk (or whenever suits you and your baby best).

Week 2: Once or twice a day

Your baby can now slurp up to about 5 spoonfuls of purée at each meal.

Week 3: Twice a day

Offer up to 10 spoonfuls at each meal – a feast!

Week 4: Two or three times a day

10 or more spoonfuls will tingle tiny taste buds at breakfast, lunch and dinner – let your baby tell you when he or she has had enough.

What to give your baby

If you do start weaning before your baby turns 6 months, start by offering a variety of pure veg, and then begin to introduce fruit and gluten-free cereals after a couple of weeks.

Once your baby is 6 months old and ready to wean, he or she can begin to enjoy puréed vegetables and fruit and cereals. From 6 months of age, little ones can eat foods that contain allergens, such as cereals containing gluten (e.g. wheat or oats), yogurt, cheese, fish or soya. Chat with your health visitor if you have allergies in the family. When you are ready, you can also offer protein foods, such as meat and pulses, as these provide an important source of iron for little ones.

Broccoli   Carrot   Peas

Parsnip   Green beans   Cauliflower

Meat   Fish   Yogurt

Wheat   Cheese

Keep up the milk

As the first steps in weaning are just about taste, it's really important that babies keep to their usual routine and amounts when it comes to milk feeds – they still need all the goodness in breast milk or formula to keep them healthy.

Remember, all little ones are different and may take to weaning differently – always be led by your baby's appetite.

From mush to mash + beyond

All babies are different. They may reach the following stages a bit earlier or later than we've suggested here, but that's totally normal. Remember that lots of the recipes in this book can be mashed up or blended for babies at 7 months onwards, too.

Look for the 'easy to mash' icon

4–5 months

Chat to your health visitor if you think your little one might be ready to wean before the age of 6 months (but after 17 weeks).

How do I eat?
I can swallow smooth, puréed food with the texture of pouring cream.

What can I eat?
Tiny tastes of a variety of smoothly puréed vegetables, followed by fruit and gluten-free cereals. Just a few spoonfuls a day.

6–7 months

How do I eat?
Using my tongue, I can move thicker purées from side to side in my mouth.

What can I eat?
A variety of vegetables and fruits. I can now eat thicker purées and can try soft finger foods, such as cooked vegetable sticks about the size of an adult's index finger. Introduce allergen foods one by one, such as cereals containing gluten, yogurt, soya, fish and eggs. Introduce protein foods, such as pulses and meat.

7–9 months

How do I eat?
I can mush up soft lumps with my tongue and I am getting better at grasping finger foods and putting them in my mouth. Let me hold a spoon and I'll try scooping.

What can I eat?
Fork-mashed fruit and veg, softly cooked minced beef and turkey, and mashed-down lentils and beans. I can eat a wider range of finger foods, such as bread or toast soldiers, scrambled egg and large pasta pieces.

10–12 months

How do I eat?
I may now have a tooth or two, so I love to munch on larger chunks. I can eat finger foods with a bit of bite and I can pick up smaller pieces of food with my pincer grip.

What can I eat?
Whole peas, beans and sweetcorn, firmer cooked veg and larger pieces of softly cooked meat, as well as raw vegetable sticks, such as cucumber or avocado.

Tiny tums and energy needs

Babies need lots of calories and nutrients to fuel their super-fast growth. In fact, per kilo of their body weight, they need more calories than you do.

However, your baby's tummy is still tiny and it can't hold a lot of food in one go. From around 10 months, it's important to give your little one three meals and two nutritious snacks each day, as well as at least 500 ml/17 fl oz of his or her usual milk.

> I use up loads of energy because I'm growing fast and learning to roll, crawl, pull myself up and even take my first tiny steps.

Handy healthy snacks

Try your baby on the following healthy snacks from around 7–9 months old, depending upon when your baby is ready.

- ☺ Pitta slices with hummus or cream cheese
- ☺ Breadsticks and dips
- ☺ Cubes of cheese
- ☺ Cooked broccoli 'trees' and carrot sticks
- ☺ Cooked pasta shapes – try the spinach and tomato varieties to provide some interesting colours

Once your baby turns 10–12 months old, blueberries, raspberries and strawberries make good snacks, too.

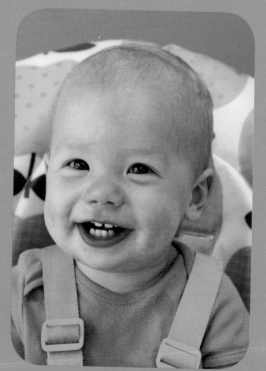

yummy lunches
+
speedy snacks

Brilliant butternut squash soup

serves
4+4
adults + kids

prep
15
minutes

cook
30–40
minutes

This soup hits the spot for a family welly walk – these children loved it. Perhaps it's the soup's sweet, rich flavour that got their senses going – or its *reeeally* bright orange colour. Add the cardamom if your little one is up for trying new flavours.

What you need

About 1.4 kg/3 lb 2 oz **butternut squash**, cut into 2.5 cm/1 in dice

Olive oil, for roasting

8 **sage** leaves, finely chopped

50 g/1¾ oz **unsalted butter**

1 **onion**, chopped

Seeds from 5 **cardamom pods**, crushed (optional)

1 litre/1¾ pints reduced-salt **vegetable stock**

Crème fraîche, to serve

Squashy tasks

Can I help?

Digging out the squash seeds with a spoon is a great way to get children involved in the early stages of the soup, as well as sprinkling over the sage before roasting. Ask your little one to watch as you blend the soup – can they see how it changes before their very eyes? Take care that the hot liquid doesn't splash, though.

What to do

1. Preheat the oven to 200°C/400°F/Gas Mark 6.

2. Put the squash cubes in a roasting tray, sprinkle with a little olive oil and scatter over the chopped sage. Toss the cubes so that they are well coated in the oil, then roast them in the oven for 15–20 minutes or until the cubes are soft and turning golden. Remove the squash from the oven and set aside.

3. Melt the butter in a large saucepan over a medium heat, then add the onion and fry until soft. Add the crushed cardamom pods (if using) and the vegetable stock. Then add the squash. Give it all a stir and bring to a boil. Reduce the heat and simmer for 15–20 minutes, until all the ingredients are soft and pulpy and the liquid has reduced a little. Remove the pan from the heat and use a hand blender to whiz the mixture until smooth.

4. Serve the soup with a small dollop of crème fraîche.

❄️ If you are freezing this dish, do so before adding the crème fraîche.

Clever tomato sauce

serves 4 · prep 15 minutes · cook 12 minutes

This sauce is clever for two reasons: first, we can think of lots of ways to use it – see opposite for four of them – and, second, it's packed to the brim with veggie goodness.

What you need

1 **carrot**, diced

200 g/7 oz **butternut squash**, diced

50 g/1¾ oz **frozen peas**, defrosted

415 g/14¾ oz can reduced-sugar and salt **baked beans**

400 g/14 oz can **chopped tomatoes**

200 g/7 oz **tomatoes**, chopped

What to do

1. In a saucepan of boiling water, boil the carrot, squash and peas for 7–8 minutes until tender, then drain and return to the pan. Keeping the pan off the heat, add the baked beans and purée the mixture with a hand blender until smooth.

2. Return the pan to the heat. Add both the canned and fresh tomatoes and bring everything to the boil. Reduce the heat and simmer for 4–5 minutes until the fresh tomatoes are soft and pulpy. Remove the pan from the heat and purée again until you have a beautifully smooth sauce.

Colour me in

Mighty grain & herby salad

Serve this crunchy salad as a side dish, or make a meal of it by topping with crumbled cheese, a boiled or poached egg, or slices of ham, cooked chicken or salmon.

What you need

60 g/2¼ oz multi-coloured **quinoa**, rinsed

1 red eating **apple**

7 cm/2¾ inch piece of **cucumber**

40 g/1½ oz **broccoli** florets, finely chopped, stalk and all

3 tablespoons finely chopped **mint leaves**

2 tablespoons finely chopped **flat-leaf parsley**

25 g/1 oz unsalted shelled **pistachio nuts,** loose skins rubbed off, finely chopped (optional)

For the dressing

Juice of 1 small **lemon**

2 tablespoons **extra virgin olive oil**

½ teaspoon **Dijon mustard**

1 teaspoon runny **honey**

What to do

1. To cook the quinoa, place it in a small saucepan and pour in enough cold water to cover by 2 cm/¾ inch. Bring to the boil, then reduce the heat and simmer, part-covered, for 15 minutes or until tender. Drain well and leave to cool for 10 minutes.

2. Meanwhile, core the apple, cut it into small bite-sized pieces, place in a serving bowl and squeeze over some of the lemon juice from the dressing ingredients. Turn the apple in the lemon juice to prevent it turning brown.

3. Halve the piece of cucumber lengthways and, using a teaspoon, scoop out and discard the seeds. Chop the rest into small bite-sized pieces and add to the apple in the bowl with the broccoli, herbs and cooled quinoa. Turn until mixed together.

4. In a small bowl or a cup, whisk together the dressing ingredients and pour over the salad, then gently turn it all around to coat. Scatter over the pistachios, if using, and serve the salad at room temperature.

Mix 'n' match

You can include everyone's favourite fruit and veggies in this flexible recipe. Instead of apple, broccoli and pistachios try equal amounts of pear, grated cauliflower and walnuts; or small chunks of Cheddar cheese, finely chopped spinach and raisins; or chopped pineapple or mango, finely chopped kale and almonds.

Seeds be gone!

Even quite small hands will love being put in charge of a teaspoon and given the job of excavating a cucumber half. Squidgy fun!

Can I help?

19

Easy cheesy courgette frittata

Getting grated courgettes into these frittatas is a simple way to sneak some good-for-you greens into a meal. The frittata is delicious warm or cold and makes a great finger food.

What you need

6 **eggs**

250 g/9 oz **Cheddar cheese**, grated

250 g/9 oz **courgette**, coarsely grated

50 g/1¾ oz **pitted black olives**, roughly chopped (optional)

3 **spring onions** or 75 g/2½ oz **leek** or **white onion**, finely chopped

Small pinch of **chilli powder** or **cayenne pepper**

1 tablespoon **olive oil**

What to do

1. Preheat the grill to medium. Crack the eggs into a large bowl and beat well using a balloon whisk. Add the Cheddar, courgette and olives (if using), the spring onions, leeks or white onion, and the chilli powder or cayenne pepper and beat again to combine.

2. Heat the oil in a 30 cm/12 inch frying pan, then pour in the egg mixture and cook over a gentle heat for 2–3 minutes until the base of the frittata is set. Place the frittata under the grill and cook for a further 3–4 minutes until the top is set and golden.

3. Slide the frittata onto a plate and cut into 8 wedges. Serve warm or cold with salad.

Go crackers!

Can I help?

Little ones can have a go at cracking the eggs into the bowl and then take a turn at beating them with a fork or balloon whisk. Who has the fastest action?

More veg

For extra veggie goodness, try adding 75 g/2½ oz of drained no-salt and no-sugar sweetcorn and/or a small, grated carrot to the bowl with the other ingredients in step 1.

Five ways with pitta, wrap or roll fillings

Bored with the same old sandwich fillings? These flavour and texture combinations put the brilliant back into bread – they are delicious, nutritious and, best of all, exciting.

Chompy cheese, carrot + apple

serves 2 · prep 5 minutes

1 tablespoon unsweetened **apple sauce** or **apple purée**

75 g/2½ oz **cream cheese**

1 tablespoon **whole milk**

1 small **carrot**, grated

50 g/1¾ oz **Cheddar cheese**, grated

¼ eating **apple**, grated

2 **pitta breads**, toasted

If you're making your own apple purée, peel, core and chop 1 eating apple. Steam it until soft, then mash with a fork.

Blend the cream cheese with the milk, then fold in 1 tablespoon of the apple sauce or purée. Stir in the carrot, Cheddar and eating apple. Make a slit in the pittas and fill them with the cheese mixture. Cut each pitta in half to serve.

Fit-for-a-king coronation chicken with mango

serves 2 · prep 5 minutes

2 tablespoons **mayonnaise**

2 tablespoons well-chopped **mango**

¼ teaspoon **medium curry powder**

150 g/5½ oz **cooked chicken breast**, torn into small pieces

50 g/1¾ oz **sultanas**

2 **flour tortillas**

2 small handfuls of **rocket**

Put the mayonnaise, mango and curry powder into a bowl and use a hand blender to combine them. Stir in the chicken and sultanas.

Spoon half the mixture in a line across the centre of 1 tortilla, then scatter over half the rocket and roll up tightly. Repeat for the other tortilla.

Cut each tortilla in half to serve.

Crumbly feta + red grape

serves 2 · prep 5 minutes

50 g/1¾ oz **feta cheese**, crumbled

25 g/1 oz finely **chopped walnuts**

1 **celery stick**, finely chopped

50 g/1¾ oz **seedless red grapes**, halved or quartered

2 tablespoons **mayonnaise**

2 **pitta breads**, toasted

Fold all the filling ingredients together in a bowl until well combined.

Make a slit in the pittas and fill with the cheese mixture. Cut each pitta in half to serve.

Sunshine hummus with basil

serves 2 · prep 5 minutes

1 **clementine**, segmented and chopped

100 g/3½ oz **hummus**

1 small **carrot**, grated

1 tablespoon shredded **basil** leaves

2 **flour tortillas**

Mix all the filling ingredients together in a bowl until well combined.

Spoon half the mixture in a line across the centre of 1 tortilla and roll the tortilla up tightly. Repeat for the other tortilla.

Cut each tortilla in half to serve.

Terrific tuna tzatziki with green grapes

serves 2 · prep 5 minutes

200 g/7 oz can **tuna steak** in spring water, drained well

4 tablespoons **tzatziki**

50 g/1¾ oz **seedless green grapes**, halved or quartered

2 **wholemeal rolls**, halved

Mix all the filling ingredients together in a bowl until well combined.

Pile half the filling into each roll. Cut in half to serve.

Dee-licious dinners

Ella's dad's sweet + sour prawns

This recipe from the Lindley family kitchen is a great introduction to the sweet and tangy savoury flavours used in recipes across Asia. We've cut the vegetables into strips, but you can slice them any way you like.

What you need

2 tablespoons **sunflower oil**

250 g/9 oz **raw tiger prawns**, patted dry

4 **spring onions**, thinly sliced

1 **red pepper**, halved, deseeded and thinly sliced

12 **baby sweetcorn**, halved lengthways

2 **carrots**, cut into thin strips

2.5 cm/1 inch piece **fresh ginger**, peeled and finely grated

2 **garlic** cloves, thinly sliced

A large handful of **bean sprouts**

For the sauce

1 tablespoon reduced-salt **light soy sauce**

2 canned **pineapple** rings in natural juice, drained and cut into chunks

2 tablespoons natural **juice from the canned pineapple** (or water)

1 tablespoon **tomato purée**

Juice of 1 **lime**

1 teaspoon **sweet chilli dipping sauce**

1 teaspoon **cornflour**

What to do

1. First make the sauce: put all the ingredients into a bowl and, using a hand blender, blend together until smooth. Set aside.

2. Heat a large wok or frying pan over a medium-high heat, add the oil and the prawns and stir-fry for 3 minutes until the prawns are pink all over. Remove the prawns with a slotted spoon and set aside.

3. Add the spring onions, red pepper, baby sweetcorn and carrots to the wok or pan and stir-fry for 2 minutes. Add the ginger and garlic and cook for another minute until the vegetables are just soft.

4. Add the sauce to the pan with 2 tablespoons water and cook for a further minute until the sauce has thickened. Return the prawns to the pan, add the bean sprouts and heat briefly. Serve immediately with noodles or rice.

 If you want to freeze this dish, make sure the prawns you use have not been pre-frozen.

That's magic!

Encourage your little ones to watch the prawns change colour as they cook – as if by magic, their dull grey becomes beautiful pink.

Five ways with green vegetables

Greens don't have to be boring. We've found the perfect partners for green beans, sprouts, broccoli, spinach and courgettes, making the most of all the natural, fresh flavours. High five if your little ones try all five!

Good-for-you green beans

serves 4 · prep 5 minutes · cook 8 minutes

300 g/10½ oz **fine green beans**, trimmed

2 tablespoons **olive oil**

3 **shallots**, finely chopped

50g/1¾ oz **pine nuts**

Cook the beans in boiling water for 5 minutes until just tender, then drain.

Meanwhile, heat the oil in a frying pan and fry the shallots for 2 minutes. Add the pine nuts and fry for 1–2 minutes. Add the cooked beans and stir-fry for 2–3 minutes to heat through. Serve immediately.

Special sprouts

serves 4 · prep 5 minutes · cook 15 minutes

350 g/12 oz **Brussels sprouts**

Unsalted butter, for frying

75 g/2½ oz **unsmoked back bacon**, chopped

1 **garlic** clove, thinly sliced

1 teaspoon **Worcestershire sauce**

Cook the sprouts in boiling water for 10 minutes until just tender, then drain.

Heat the butter in a frying pan and fry the bacon and garlic for 3 minutes until golden. Add the sprouts and fry for 1 minute to heat through, then add the Worcestershire sauce and stir-fry for a few seconds before serving immediately.

Brilliant broccoli

serves 4 | prep 5 minutes | cook 8 minutes

300 g/10½ oz **broccoli florets**

1 tablespoon **toasted sesame oil**

1 tablespoon **sesame seeds**

1 tablespoon reduced-salt **light soy sauce**

Cook the broccoli in boiling water for 4–5 minutes until just tender, then drain.

Heat the oil in a frying pan and toast the sesame seeds for 1 minute until golden. Add the cooked broccoli and the soy sauce and stir-fry, tossing for 1 minute to heat through. Serve immediately.

Splendid spinach

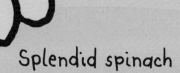

serves 4 | prep 5 minutes | cook 5 minutes

1 kg/2 lb 4 oz packet **frozen spinach**

A pinch of **ground nutmeg**

4 tablespoons **crème fraîche**

1 tablespoon grated **Parmesan cheese**

Cook the spinach in a saucepan according to the packet instructions. Drain and press out as much of the liquid as possible, then return the spinach to the pan.

Add the remaining ingredients and stir to combine. Serve immediately.

Cracking courgettes

serves 4 | prep 5 minutes | cook 7 minutes

1 tablespoon **olive oil**

450 g/1 lb **courgettes**, halved lengthways and sliced

Juice and finely grated zest of ½ **lemon**

A handful of **basil** leaves, finely chopped

Heat the oil in a frying pan and fry the courgettes for 5–6 minutes until golden and just tender.

Remove from the heat and stir in the lemon zest and juice and the basil. Serve immediately.

Ella's mum's easy chicken curry

serves **4** · prep **10** minutes · cook **30** minutes

Ella's mum first made this when Ella was just three years old – and Ella has been enjoying it ever since. It is a mild, sweet and creamy curry that's guaranteed to get tiny taste buds tingling with all the spices of exotic adventure.

What you need

2 tablespoons **olive oil**

1 small **onion**, chopped

2 **garlic** cloves, crushed

2 **chicken breasts** (about 300 g/10½ oz), cut into bite-sized pieces

2 cm/¾ inch piece **fresh ginger**, grated

1 teaspoon **mild curry powder**

1 small **sweet potato**, diced

250 g/9 oz **carrots**, sliced

250 ml/9 fl oz **light coconut milk**

100 ml/3½ fl oz reduced-salt **vegetable stock**

1 small **mango**, cut into chunks

125 g/4½ oz **green beans**, trimmed

2 tablespoons finely chopped **flat-leaf parsley**

What to do

1. Heat the oil in a large saucepan and add the onion and garlic. Fry for 1 minute, stirring, then add the chicken pieces and cook for 3–4 minutes over a medium heat, stirring every now and then until the chicken pieces are golden brown all over.

2. Add the grated ginger and the curry powder and cook for a further minute, stirring all the time. Add the sweet potato and carrots, then pour in the coconut milk and stock, and add the mango. Mix everything together well and bring the liquid to the boil. Cover, reduce the heat to low and simmer, stirring occasionally, for 20 minutes until the sweet potato is soft.

3. Add the beans and cook for a further 3 minutes until the beans are just soft. Finally, stir in the parsley. Serve immediately on a bed of rice or with a naan bread.

Ella's shortcut

To save some time on chopping, you can substitute a 90g/3¼ oz pouch of Ella's Kitchen Smoothie Fruits – The Yellow One for the chunks of mango.

Colour me in

Kids' kedgeree

serves **6** | prep **10** minutes | cook **25** minutes

This yummy tea introduces kids to kedgeree without the need for the strong smoked-fish flavour and with only a little curry powder (fun for tiny taste buds).

What you need

350 g/12 oz **cod fillet**, skinned

300 ml/½ pint **whole milk**

50 g/1¾ oz **unsalted butter**

1 **onion**, finely chopped

½ teaspoon **cayenne pepper**

1 teaspoon **mild curry powder**

300 g/10½ oz **easy-cook long grain rice**

1 litre/1¾ pints reduced-salt **chicken stock** or water

150 g/5½ oz **frozen peas**, defrosted

150 g/5½ oz **frozen sweetcorn**, defrosted

4 **eggs**, hard-boiled and roughly chopped

2 tablespoons finely chopped **flat-leaf parsley**

What to do

1. Put the cod in a deep frying pan with the milk, bring to the boil, then reduce the heat to low and simmer uncovered for 5 minutes, or until cooked through.

2. Using a slotted spoon, transfer the fish to a bowl, reserving the warm milk. Flake the fish with a fork, taking care to remove any bones.

3. Melt the butter in a medium saucepan. Add the onion and cayenne pepper and cook for 2–3 minutes until the onion is beginning to soften. Add the curry powder and cook for a further minute.

4. Add the rice and stir to coat it in the oil. Pour in the chicken stock and the reserved milk and bring to the boil. Reduce the heat to low, cover and simmer for 10–15 minutes until the rice is cooked and almost all the stock and milk have been absorbed. Add the peas and the sweetcorn, stir thoroughly and cook for a further 2 minutes.

5. Carefully fold in the flaked fish and eggs. Sprinkle with the chopped parsley.

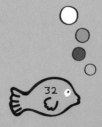

32

Zingy lamb + couscous with mangoes + raisins

serves **6** prep **15** minutes cook **1¼** hours

omit green beans

Packed full of flavoursome fruit and veg, this couscous dish really does zing!

What you need

2 tablespoons **olive oil**

1 **garlic** clove, crushed

350 g/12 oz **lamb leg fillet**, diced

1 **onion**, chopped

2 teaspoons **ground cumin**

½ teaspoon **ground cinnamon**

1 **carrot**, diced

350 g/12 oz **butternut squash**, diced

400 g/14 oz can **chopped tomatoes**

500 ml/17 fl oz reduced-salt **vegetable stock**

1 small, ripe **mango**, chopped into small pieces

100 g/3½ oz **green beans**, cut into 1 cm/½ inch pieces

200 g/7 oz **couscous**

50 g/1¾ oz **raisins** (optional)

What to do

1. Preheat the oven to 180°C/350°F/Gas Mark 4.

2. Heat the oil in a frying pan and fry the garlic, lamb, onion and spices for 5 minutes until the lamb has browned on all sides. Transfer the mixture to a casserole dish.

3. Put the carrot and squash in the frying pan and cook for 3–4 minutes until softened, then add the tomatoes and 300 ml/½ pint of the stock and bring the mixture to the boil.

4. As soon as the tomato and stock mixture starts to boil, remove it from the heat and stir it into the lamb. Add the chopped mango, give it all another stir, then cover and bake in the oven for 1½ hours until the lamb is tender.

5. Once the lamb is ready, boil the green beans in the remaining stock for 2–3 minutes until just tender. Remove the beans from the liquid with a slotted spoon and set aside. Pour the stock into a measuring jug and set aside.

6. Put the couscous and raisins (if using) into a heatproof bowl and add the beans. Check how much stock you have in the measuring jug – you'll need 200 ml/7 fl oz, so top up with some boiling water if necessary. Pour the liquid over the couscous. Cover with clingflim and leave for 5 minutes until absorbed. Fluff the couscous with a fork and serve with the lamb.

❄ The couscous is unsuitable for freezing, but pop the lamb into the freezer for another day.

Squishy salmon fishcakes

serves **2+2** adults + kids

prep **20** minutes + cooling

cook **25** minutes

omit green beans

Break out your artistic side and create lots of squishy fishy goodness with lots of squishy fishy style.

What you need

400 g/14 oz **potatoes**, cut into large dice

1 **carrot**, cut into small dice

200 g/7 oz **salmon fillets**, skin removed

3 tablespoons **sunflower oil**

1 small **leek,** thinly sliced

25 g/1 oz **green beans,** finely chopped

2 tablespoons finely chopped **flat-leaf parsley**

Blowing bubbles

Turn the plate into a work of art – ask your little one to arrange a few peas as if the fishy fishcakes were blowing bubbles.

What to do

1. Cook the potato and carrot in boiling water for 15 minutes until tender. Drain and mash them together, then set aside to cool.

2. Meanwhile, poach the salmon in simmering water for 5 minutes until cooked through, then lift out and allow to cool. Break the fish into flakes, taking care to ensure that there are no bones.

3. Heat 1 tablespoon of the oil in a large frying pan and fry the leek and beans for 5 minutes until tender. Stir them into the carrot and potato mash, then add the cooked salmon and the parsley to the mixture and stir again.

4. Using your hands, mould the mixture into 2 large fishcakes and 2 smaller fishcakes. (Fishy shapes look great.)

5. Heat the remaining oil in a frying pan and cook the fishcakes for 5 minutes, turning once, until golden on both sides and heated through. Serve immediately with some peas.

Colour us in

Five ways with potatoes

Who knew potatoes could be so tasty? Gone are the days of bland school mash. Encourage little ones to make shapes from the potato peelings – or see who can peel the longest strip (under supervision, of course).

Rosemary roasties

serves 6 · prep 10 minutes · cook 1 hour

700 g/1 lb 9 oz **King Edward potatoes**, cut into large chunks

3 tablespoons **sunflower oil**

1 tablespoon **rosemary** leaves

Preheat the oven to 200°C/400°F/Gas Mark 6. Place the potatoes in a large saucepan, cover them with water, bring them to the boil, then reduce the heat to low and simmer for 10 minutes. Drain well and return the potatoes to the pan.

Add the oil and shake the pan a little to coat the potato cubes. Transfer them to a baking tray, drizzle over any excess oil left in the pan and sprinkle over the rosemary. Bake in the oven for 45–55 minutes until golden and crispy, turning the chunks after 30 minutes to make sure they go crispy all over.

Herby mash up

serves 6 · prep 10 minutes · cook 15 minutes

700 g/1 lb 9 oz **floury potatoes**, cut into chunks

50 g/1¾ oz **unsalted butter**

2 **garlic** cloves, crushed

50 ml/2 fl oz **whole milk**

2 tablespoons finely chopped **flat-leaf parsley**, or 4 tablespoons **crème fraîche** and 2 tablespoons chopped **chives** (optional)

Put the potatoes in a large saucepan, cover them with water, bring them to the boil, then reduce the heat to low and simmer for 10–15 minutes until tender. Drain well.

Put the empty pan back on the heat. Melt the butter and add the garlic, then fry it for 1 minute until soft. Remove the pan from the heat. Add the potatoes and the milk and mash well, then stir in the parsley.

Alternatively, mash the potatoes with the milk and stir in the crème fraîche and chopped chives in place of the parsley.

38

Baby jackets

serves 6 · prep 2 minutes · cook 45 minutes

700 g/1 lb 9 oz **new potatoes**

1 tablespoon **olive oil**

Preheat the oven to 200°C/400°F/Gas Mark 6.

Place the potatoes on a baking tray and sprinkle over the oil. Toss to coat evenly. Bake for 45 minutes or until golden and cooked all the way through.

Sweet potato fishy chips

serves 6 · prep 5 minutes · cook 30 minutes

700 g/1 lb 9 oz **sweet potatoes**, thickly sliced

1 tablespoon **sunflower oil**

2 tablespoons **maple syrup**

Preheat the oven to 200°C/400°F/Gas Mark 6. Use a fish-shaped cutter to cut your sweet-potato slices into fishy chips. Put them in a large roasting tin, add the oil and maple syrup and toss to coat. Bake for 25–30 minutes until tender, turning once.

Cheesy chips

serves 6 · prep 2 minutes · cook 25 minutes

700 g/1 lb 9 oz **oven chips**

75 g/2½ oz **Cheddar cheese**, grated

Preheat the oven to 220°C/425°F/Gas Mark 7. Spread the chips out on a large baking tray and cook for 20–25 minutes, or according to the packet instructions, until golden. Sprinkle over the Cheddar. Toss well until the cheese has melted slightly, then return to the oven for 1 minute.

Slurp me

Marvellous meatballs

makes **24**   prep **10** minutes   cook **15** minutes

This basic mixture will make handfuls of meatballs that are ideal for play-date dinners. We've served them here with our Clever Tomato Sauce.

What you need

500 g/1 lb 2 oz **lean minced pork**

25 g/1 oz **breadcrumbs**

2 teaspoons **dried thyme**

2 teaspoons **Dijon mustard**

1½ teaspoons **Worcestershire sauce**

1 **garlic** clove, crushed

1 tablespoon **vegetable oil**

Freshly ground **black pepper**

What to do

1. Put the pork in a large mixing bowl and break it up using a fork. Stir in the rest of the ingredients, except the oil and pepper, first with a fork and then with your hands to mix everything together well. Season with black pepper and mix again.

2. Form the mixture into 24 mini meatballs, each about the size of a walnut.

3. Heat the oil in a large frying pan over a medium heat. Add the meatballs and fry for 15 minutes, reducing the heat to low if they start to become too dark, turning occasionally, until cooked through and golden. (You may need to do this in batches, in which case set each batch aside on a warm plate as it is cooked.)

4. Serve the meatballs on a mound of spaghetti topped with lashings of our Clever Tomato Sauce (see page 16).

❄ These meatballs can be frozen before or after they are cooked.

Three easy pasta sauces

These three pasta sauces are packed full of good, tasty stuff and can be stirred into any shape, size or colour of pasta. We've suggested which pasta to use, but why not try some different types, and see which you like best?

Lemony pea + mint pasta

serves 4–6 | prep 10 minutes | cook 15 minutes

What you need

1 tablespoon **olive oil**, plus extra for drizzling (optional)

1 large **onion**, chopped

1 **courgette**, chopped

200 g/7 oz **frozen peas**

2 **garlic** cloves, finely chopped

½ teaspoon low-salt **vegetable bouillon** powder

A handful of **mint leaves** (about 5 g/⅛ oz)

Squeeze of **lemon** juice

Freshly ground **black pepper**

Parmesan cheese, grated, to serve

8 cherry **tomatoes**, diced, to serve

What to do

1. Heat the olive oil in a large frying pan over a medium-low heat, add the onion and cook gently, stirring often, for 5 minutes. Add the courgette, peas and garlic and cook for another 10 minutes until softened.

2. Meanwhile, cook some conchiglie (shells) pasta according to the packet instructions.

3. Using a hand blender, blend the pea mixture with 150 ml/5 fl oz of the pasta cooking water (ladle it out as the pasta cooks), the bouillon powder and mint until smooth and creamy. Add a squeeze of lemon juice and season with pepper.

4. Serve the green sauce stirred into the pasta, topped with Parmesan, diced tomatoes and a final drizzle of olive oil, if you like.

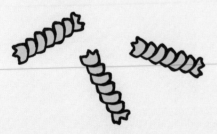

Turkey bolognese

serves 4–6 | prep 10 minutes | cook 35 minutes

What you need

2 tablespoons **olive oil**

1 large **onion**, finely chopped

1 **celery** stick, finely chopped

1 **carrot**, finely chopped

2 large **garlic** cloves, finely chopped

300 g/10½ oz **minced turkey**

1 teaspoon **dried oregano**

1 tablespoon **tomato purée**

400 g/14 oz can chopped **tomatoes**

185 ml/6 fl oz reduced-salt **beef stock**

Freshly ground **black pepper**

What to do

1. Heat the oil in a large saucepan over a medium heat. Add the onion and cook, stirring often, for 5 minutes. Reduce the heat slightly, add the celery and carrot and cook for another 5 minutes, covered, until the vegetables are tender.

2. Stir in the garlic and minced turkey and cook for 5 minutes, stirring to break up the meat, until it turns white and all trace of pink has gone.

3. Add the oregano, tomato purée, chopped tomatoes and stock and bring to the boil. Reduce the heat and simmer, part-covered with a lid, for 20 minutes, until the mince is cooked and the sauce has reduced and thickened. Season with pepper and serve over tagliatelle.

Big red tomato pesto

serves 4–6 | prep 15 minutes | cook 30 minutes

What you need

400 g/14 oz **tomatoes**, halved or quartered

4 **garlic** cloves, skins left on

2 tablespoons **extra virgin olive oil** (or oil from the jar of sun-dried tomatoes), plus extra for drizzling

25 g/1 oz **Brazil nuts**, roughly chopped

40 g/1½ oz **sun-dried tomatoes**, drained and roughly chopped

20 g/¾ oz **Parmesan** cheese, grated, plus extra for sprinkling

Freshly ground **black pepper**

Basil leaves, to serve

What to do

1. Preheat the oven to 200°C/400°F/Gas Mark 6. Put the tomatoes and garlic on a large baking tray and drizzle over a little olive oil. Toss well, then roast for 25–30 minutes until the tomatoes start to break down and the garlic is tender.

2. Finely chop the nuts in a food processor. Add the roasted tomatoes, dried tomatoes and oil. Squeeze each garlic clove out of its skin (discard the skin), add to the processor and blitz to a coarse paste. Season with pepper and stir in the Parmesan.

3. Cook some penne pasta according to the packet instructions. Stir 100 ml/3½ fl oz of the cooking water (ladle it out as the pasta cooks) into the pesto. Drain the pasta, return to the pan and stir in the pesto, some extra Parmesan and the basil leaves.

Full-of-sunshine Thai curry

serves 4 prep 10 minutes cook 18 minutes

Bursting with bright colours, this gentle introduction to Thai flavours provides plenty of adventure for tiny taste buds.

What you need

1 tablespoon **vegetable oil**

400 g/14 oz **butternut squash**, diced

1 large **onion**, diced

1 **carrot**, sliced

1 **red pepper**, deseeded and sliced

100 g/3½ oz **sugar snap peas**

3 cm/1¼ inch piece **root ginger**, grated

1 **garlic** clove, crushed

1 teaspoon **ground cumin**

½ teaspoon **mild chilli powder**

400 ml/14 fl oz can **coconut milk**

1 reduced-salt **vegetable stock cube**, crumbled

A large handful of **coriander**, finely chopped

4 **lime** wedges, to serve (optional)

What to do

1. Heat the oil in a large frying pan and cook the squash, onion and carrot for 5 minutes unil the onion is soft. Add the pepper, sugar snap peas, ginger, garlic and spices and fry for 2–3 minutes, stirring occasionally.

2. Stir in the coconut milk and crumbled stock cube, cover and simmer for 10 minutes, stirring occasionally, until the vegetables are tender. Stir in the coriander.

3. Serve the curry with basmati rice, and lime wedges (if using).

Thai-taste-tastic!

Thai food is famously fragrant, which makes this a fab meal for encouraging your toddler to explore how smell and taste work together. Offer up the cut ginger root and a few coriander leaves for a sniff-fest. Talk about the different smells. Can your toddler taste those smells when he or she tucks into the bowl of cooked curry?

Perfect puds
+
scrummy treats

Baby baked apples

makes 8 · prep 15 minutes · cook 40 minutes

A favourite winter pud, the mini apples are filled with a cinnamon and fruit butter, then baked until lovely and soft.

What you need

60 g/2¼ oz stoned **dates**

8 mini eating **apples**, washed and dried

50 g/1¾ oz **unsalted butter,** softened

1 teaspoon **ground cinnamon**

1 teaspoon **vanilla extract**

40 g/1½ oz **raisins**

Juice of ½ **orange**

What to do

1. Put the dates in a small heatproof bowl. Pour over enough just-boiled water from a kettle to cover, then leave to soak for 20 minutes until softened. Drain the dates, throwing away the soaking water, then chop them.

2. Preheat the oven to 180°C/350°F/Gas Mark 4. Cut a triangular-shaped cavity from each apple, removing most of the core at the same time but keeping the bottom intact. Cut a sliver from the base if the apples won't stand up, then score around the circumference with a sharp knife to stop them splitting.

3. Using a hand blender, blend the butter, chopped dates, cinnamon and vanilla until combined. Stir in the raisins. Fill each of the apples with the raisin butter, pressing the mixture into the cavities.

4. Place the apples in a baking dish, spoon over the orange juice and cover with foil. Bake for 40 minutes until the apples are soft but not collapsing, removing the foil halfway through to spoon over the buttery juices in the tin. Serve with spoonfuls of crème fraîche or Greek yogurt.

Can I help?

Squeeeeezy juicy

Whether you have a citrus press or a hand citrus juicer, pressing down on the flesh of the orange and watching the delicious juice come out is pure culinary magic for little ones. Put the juice in a measuring jug to see how much you managed to squeeze out.

Scrummy

Mmmminty green lollies

serves 6 · prep 10 minutes

No one will guess the secret ingredient in these refreshing, creamy lollies. Make sure the avocado (shhh!) and bananas are perfectly ripe for the best flavour. If not using peppermint extract, add an extra tablespoon of finely chopped mint leaves, though the lollies won't be quite so minty.

What you need

1 ripe **avocado**

2 ripe **bananas**, peeled and sliced

⅓ teaspoon pure **peppermint extract,** or to taste (optional)

200 ml/7 fl oz **coconut water**

1 tablespoon finely chopped **mint leaves**, plus extra if needed

1 tablespoon runny **honey**, or to taste

Juice of 2 **limes**

What to do

1. Halve the avocado, take out the stone, then scoop the flesh into a blender.

2. Add the bananas plus all the other ingredients and blend until smooth and creamy. If you didn't use peppermint extract, add an extra tablespoon of finely chopped mint leaves.

3. Taste and make sure you are happy with the level of sweetness and minty flavour, adding more honey or peppermint extract if you want. When frozen, the flavours in the mixture will be muted, so be brave!

4. Pour the mixture into 6 lolly moulds and freeze for at least 6 hours, or preferably overnight, until firm.

51

Zingy pineapple with basil + lime

These ingredients sound quite grown up, but we've found that older toddlers are interested to find out about the zesty tastes and textures – and then love them when they tuck in.

What you need

Juice and finely grated zest of 1 **lime**

50 g/1¾ oz **soft dark brown sugar**

1 tablespoon finely chopped **basil** leaves

1 whole **pineapple**, peeled, cored and cut into 'soldier'-like slices

What to do

1. Place the lime zest and juice in a bowl and stir in the sugar and basil. Leave the mixture to marinate for 5 minutes until the sugar has dissolved to form a syrup.

2. Arrange the pineapple 'soldiers' on a large serving plate and drizzle over some of the lime and basil syrup. Put any remaining syrup in a little bowl for extra dunking. Serve immediately.

Smell-a-thon

Crushing the basil releases its delicious smell – talk to your toddler about it and what it might remind you of. Summertime? Pizza? And what about the smell of the lime? How is that different from the pineapple?

Make it mango

As an alternative, you can replace the pineapple with 2 peeled and sliced fresh mangoes for a different kind of tropical flavour.

Fabulous fruit compote

serves 8 · prep 10 minutes · cook 20 minutes

You can enjoy this versatile fruit compote for breakfast served with yogurt and granola, as a hot or cold snack, or for a dinnertime pud served with ice cream or custard.

What you need

2 eating **apples**, peeled, cored and diced

2 **Conference pears**, peeled, cored and diced

350 g/12 oz **plums**, stoned and diced

75 g/2½ oz **dried prunes**, roughly chopped

50 g/1¾ oz **sultanas**

Juice and finely grated zest of 1 **orange**

½ teaspoon **ground mixed spice**

What to do

1. Place all the ingredients in a medium saucepan, cover with a lid and cook gently for 20 minutes, stirring occasionally, until the fruit has softened but there is still some texture.

2. Remove the pan from the heat. Serve the compote warm or cold.

Hello...

Teeny weeny fruit muffins

makes **12**   prep **15** minutes   cook **35** minutes

The fruit purée makes these muffins reeeally moist. They are easy peasy to make and bake in 20 minutes, so they provide a perfect afternoon cooking activity when a friend comes to play. Mmmm…warm muffins to keep them going until tea. Perfect!

What you need

75 g/2½ oz **unsalted butter**

75 g/2½ oz **strawberries**, hulled

125 g/4½ oz **bananas** (about 2) sliced

1 **egg**

1 teaspoon **vanilla extract**

100 g/3½ oz **self-raising wholemeal flour**

¾ teaspoon **baking powder**

50 g/1¾ oz **raisins**

40 g/1½ oz **walnuts**, chopped (optional)

Porridge oats, for sprinkling

What to do

1) Preheat the oven to 180°C/350°F/Gas Mark 4. Line a mini muffin tin with paper cake cases.

2) Melt the butter in a small saucepan, then leave to cool slightly.

3) Using a hand blender, whiz the strawberries and bananas together in a bowl until almost smooth.

4) Pour the fruit purée into a mixing bowl and beat in the melted butter, the egg and vanilla. Sift in the flour and baking powder and stir again. Finally, stir in the raisins and walnuts (if using).

5) Divide the mixture between the cake cases, filling each one three-quarters full so that the muffins have room to rise. Sprinkle a few porridge oats over each muffin.

6) Bake for 30–35 minutes, or until the muffins are firm to the touch and golden on top. Cool on a wire rack before serving. They will keep in an airtight container for up to 3 days.

Bake away!

> Can I help?

This is a baking extravaganza for tiny helpers. Little ones can get stuck in with the egg-cracking, the sifting, the stirring and the sprinkling – so much to do, so much messy fun to be had.

Rise 'n' shine banana bread

makes **10** slices   prep **10** minutes   cook **40** minutes

This simple banana bread is deliciously moist and ideal for a late breakfast, as a snack for a trip to the park, or with a cup of juice mid-afternoon.

What you need

310 g/11 oz ripe **bananas**, mashed

2 tablespoons **agave syrup**

3 **eggs**

250 g/9 oz **self-raising flour**

1 teaspoon **baking powder**

1 teaspoon **bicarbonate of soda**

25 g/1 oz **butter**, cubed

What to do

1. Preheat the oven to 160°C/325°F/Gas Mark 3. Lightly oil a 900 g/2 lb loaf tin.

2. Put the mashed banana, agave syrup and eggs in a bowl and use a wooden spoon to beat them together until well combined.

3. In a separate large bowl, sift together the flour, baking powder and bicarbonate of soda, then use your fingertips to rub in the butter until the mixture resembles fine breadcrumbs.

4. Tip the egg and banana mixture into the dry ingredients and mix them together until well combined. Spoon the mixture into the prepared loaf tin and level the top. Bake for 1–1¼ hours until well risen and golden, and hollow-sounding when you tap the base.

5. Cool the loaf in the tin, then turn it out and cut into slices to serve.

Awesome orange + ginger cake

This cake is a sweet and scrummy introduction to ginger – have fun helping your little ones discover new flavours for their developing taste buds.

What you need

175 g/6 oz **unsalted butter,** plus extra for greasing

150 g/5½ oz **golden syrup**

225 g/8 oz **self-raising flour**

2 teaspoons **ground ginger**

1 teaspoon **ground cinnamon**

190 g/6¾ oz **orange marmalade**

2 **eggs**, lightly beaten

2 tablespoons **whole milk**

What to do

1. Preheat the oven to 180°C/350°F/Gas Mark 4. Grease a 20 cm/8 inch square cake tin and line the base with baking parchment.

2. Melt the butter and syrup in a small saucepan over a low heat, stirring well to combine. Remove the mixture from the heat and set aside.

3. Sift the flour, ginger and cinnamon in a large mixing bowl, then slowly pour the syrup mixture into the bowl, stirring with a wooden spoon until combined. Beat the marmalade into the eggs and milk in a jug and stir into the cake mixture until the batter is smooth.

4. Pour the mixture into the cake tin, spreading it out evenly if necessary, and bake for 40–45 minutes until golden and firm to the touch. It is ready when a skewer inserted into the middle of the cake comes out clean.

5. Allow the cake to cool for 15 minutes in the tin before carefully removing it to a wire rack. Cut the cake into squares and serve warm or cold, with a spoonful of thick natural yogurt or a scoop of vanilla ice cream.

Purple pancakes

makes 12 | prep 10 minutes | cook 8 minutes

Who said pancakes have to be yellow? Squished blueberries added to the batter make pancakes that are purple – a special surprise for the weekend.

150 g/5½ oz **self-raising flour**

1 **egg**

150 ml/¼ pint **whole milk**

50 g/1¾ oz **blueberries**

Unsalted butter, for frying

Maple syrup, to serve (optional)

Fresh fruit, to serve (optional)

Sift the flour into a small mixing bowl and make a well in the centre.

Break the egg into a jug, add the milk, and mix well. Pour the mixture into the well and, using a balloon whisk, draw the flour into the liquid gradually and mix it all together until combined to a smooth batter.

Place the blueberries in a small bowl and, using a hand blender, whiz until almost smooth and very purple!

Pour the purple purée into the pancake batter and mix well.

Wipe the base of a large, heavy-based frying pan with a little butter and heat. Pour large spoonfuls of the batter, spaced well apart, into the the pan and cook the pancakes for about 1 minute, then flip them over using a fish slice and cook for 30–60 seconds more until golden brown on both sides.

Transfer the pancakes to a plate and keep them warm. Repeat the process until all the batter is used up. Serve the pancakes warm with a little maple syrup and fresh fruit (if using).

Scale school

Can I help?

Measuring out the blueberries is a good introduction for little ones to using scales – and less messy than measuring out flour or sugar!

Holey moley pancakes

This is a variation on pikelets, courtesy of Kim who runs our Making Friends team here at Ella's Kitchen. She loves to make them with her nieces and nephews when they come to stay. The little holes are the secret to a great pancake taste experience.

125 g/4½ oz **plain flour**

½ teaspoon **baking soda**

½ teaspoon **cream of tartar**

1 **egg**

1 tablespoon **sugar**

25 g/1 oz **unsalted butter**, melted, plus extra for frying

150 ml/¼ pint **whole milk**

Fresh fruit, to serve (optional)

Mix the flour with the baking powder and cream of tartar. In a separate bowl, whisk the egg and sugar, then stir in the melted butter. Then, alternately add small amounts of the flour mixture and the milk to the egg mixture until everything is combined to a thick batter.

Wipe the base of a large, heavy-based frying pan with a little butter and heat. Spoon in individual tablespoons of the batter to form small pancakes. Cook for about 1 minute until the bubbles have burst, then flip the pancakes over using a fish slice and cook for 30 seconds more until golden brown on both sides.

Transfer the pancakes to a plate and keep them warm. Repeat the process until all the batter is used up. Serve the pancakes warm with fresh fruit (if using).